Newcastle
City Council

Newcastle Libraries and Information Service

☎ **0191 277 4100**

12/04

Due for return	Due for return	Due for return
13 APR 2007		
-2 NOV 2007		
-2 NOV 2007		
-6 MAY 2009		

Please return this item to any of Newcastle's Libraries by the last
date shown above. If not requested by another customer the loan
can be renewed, you can do this by phone, post or in person.
Charges may be made for late returns.

Signs of
Spring

Paul Humphrey
Photography by Chris Fairclough

W
FRANKLIN WATTS
LONDON • SYDNEY

This edition 2006

First published in Great Britain by
Franklin Watts
338 Euston Road
London NW1 3BH

Franklin Watts Australia
Hachette Children's Books
Level 17/207 Kent Street
Sydney NSW 2000

© 2001 Franklin Watts

ISBN-10: 0 7496 6954 3
ISBN-13: 978 0 7496 6954 6

Dewey Decimal Classification: 574.5
A CIP catalogue record for this book is available from the British Library

Printed in China

Planning and production by Discovery Books
Editors: Tamsin Osler, Samantha Armstrong
Design: Ian Winton
Art Director: Jonathan Hair

Photographs:
Bruce Coleman: 9 (Kim Taylor), 18 (George McCarthy), 19 (Robert Maier),
20 (Kim Taylor), 21 (Jorg & Petra Wegner), 23 (Kim Taylor); Alex Ramsay/Discovery
Books Picture Library: 28; Tony Stone Images: 13 (Peter Cade).
All other photography by Chris Fairclough.

'I Planted Some Seeds' from THERE'S AN AWFUL LOT OF WEIRDOS
IN OUR NEIGHBOURHOOD © 1987 Colin McNaughton.
Reproduced by permission of the publisher, Walker Books Ltd, London.

CONTENTS

Spring is here.
Look for the signs of spring.

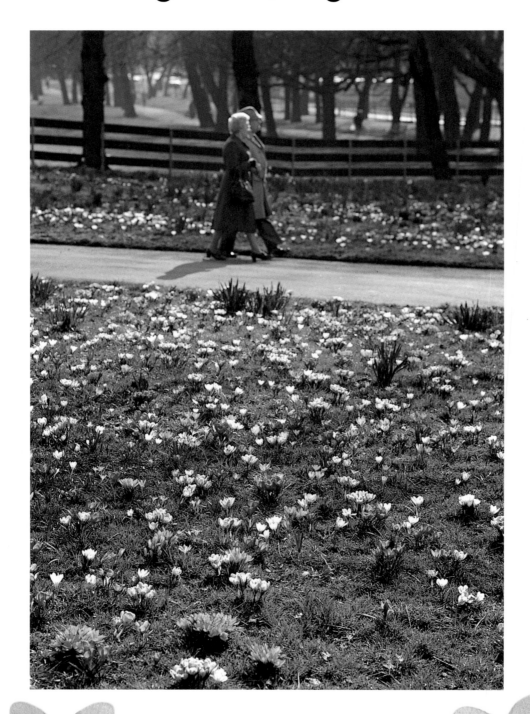

The days are getting warmer.

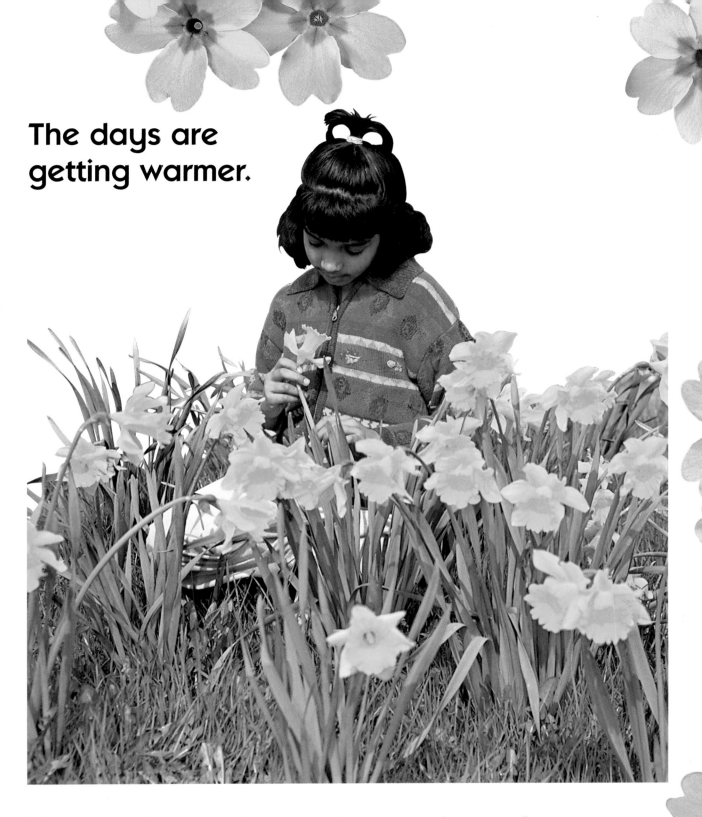

You don't need your hat and scarf anymore.

You can open your window...

...and listen to the
birds singing outside.

At school you do spring projects.

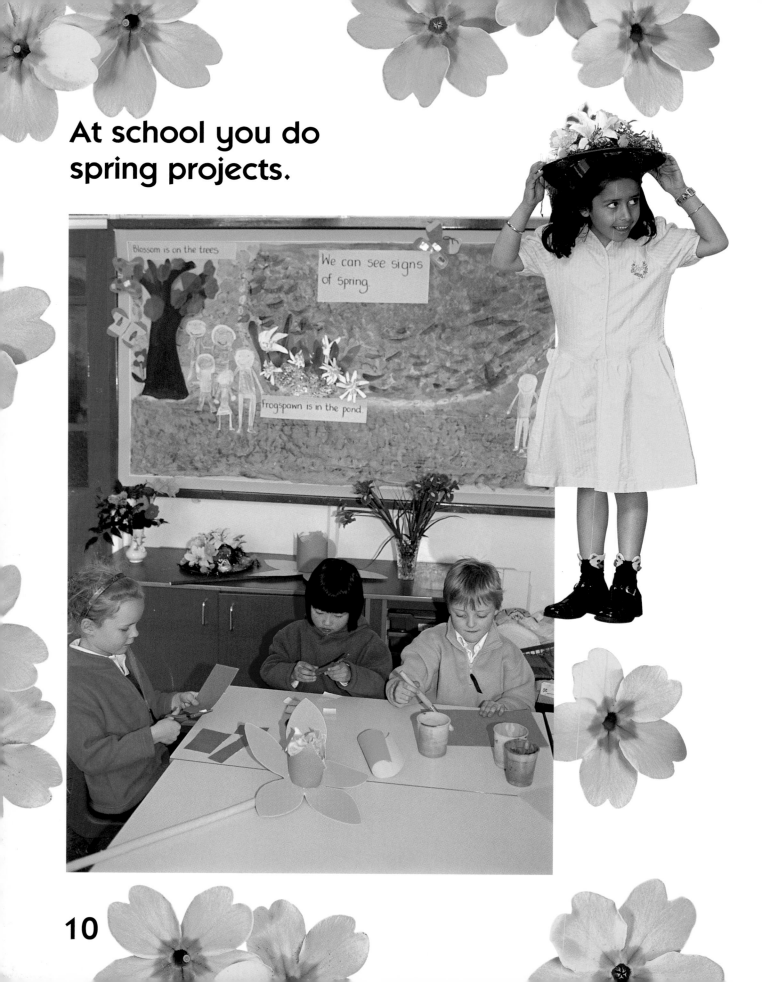

Blossom is on the trees

We can see signs of spring

Frogspawn is in the pond

It stays lighter in the evenings, so you can play outside after school.

Sometimes it is sunny. Sometimes it is wet.

You often see rainbows in spring.

Sometimes it is windy.

13

There are new leaves
on some trees...

14

...and many trees are covered in blossom.

The daffodils are flowering...

...and so are the bluebells.

Some animals are waking up from
their winter sleep.

18

They look for insects and grubs to eat.

The swallows have come back.

All the birds are making their nests.

There is frog spawn in the school pond.

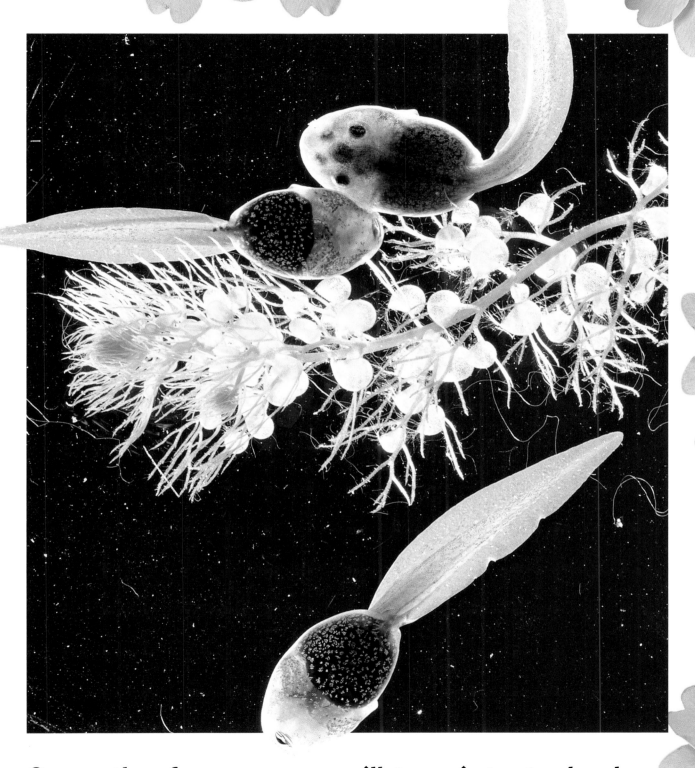

Soon the frog spawn will turn into tadpoles.

Lambs are born
in the spring...

...so are calves.

You can plant herbs and vegetables
ready for the summer...

...but you will have to watch out for slugs and snails!

What other signs of spring can you see?

I Planted Some Seeds

I planted some seeds
In my garden today.
They haven't come up yet,
I hope they're okay.

Should I dig them all up,
Take them back to the shop?
Ask for my money back,
Say they're a flop?

Perhaps they were faulty,
Perhaps they were duff,
Maybe they haven't
Been watered enough.

I planted some seeds
In my garden today.
They haven't come up yet,
I hope they're okay.

Colin McNaughton

INDEX